Grandpa and the Peahen

Written and Illustrated by
Terry Ann Buchanan

Copyright © 2020 by Terry Ann Buchanan
Book design by Faith Buchanan

All rights reserved. No part of this book may be used or reproduced in any matter whatsoever without the written permission from the author.
For permission contact: terryannbuchanan20@gmail.com

ISBN: 978-0-578-77798-6

Any references to real people or places are used fictitiously.
Names, characters, and places are products of the author's imagination.

Printed in the United States of America
First printing edition 2020

In loving memory of Ken,
who inspired me to write this story.

With love to my daughter, Faith,
for editing and designing my book.
With special thanks to Mary,
for all your editing and encouragement.

Grandpa lived in a farmhouse in the country. It was springtime, and Grandpa loved to work in his garden.

He had a grandson called Little Matt. Every day after school, Little Matt visited Grandpa and helped him in the garden.

One afternoon, Grandpa saw a strange bird wandering behind his garden.

"Look over yonder, Little Matt," Grandpa said.

"Is that a peacock over there?" said Little Matt.

"Well," said Grandpa, "the male is a peacock, but she's called a peahen."

Little Matt said, "Well, Grandpa, she must be the queen of the peahens 'cause she's wearing a crown."

The next day, Little Matt spotted the peahen and saw something very special.

"Look, Grandpa, the peahen has a baby chick!"

"Yes, indeed," Grandpa said. "It's her peachick."

Wherever mama peahen pranced, her little peachick followed.

When mama peahen squawked, her little peachick chirped, "Peep, peep, peep!"

With sweet satisfaction, Grandpa said, "Little wonders are everywhere."

Every day, Grandpa and Little Matt saw the peahen and her peachick near the garden.

Then one cloudy afternoon, they heard a loud cry. They saw the peahen moaning. She was all alone.

Little Matt said, "Grandpa, what's wrong with our peahen?"

"Well ... it looks like ... she is very sad because something has happened to her peachick."

Grandpa and Little Matt searched the garden for her peachick but couldn't find it.

Every day as Grandpa pulled those pesky weeds, he wondered how the sadness could be pulled out of mama peahen's heart.

One morning, while he gathered eggs from his chickens and ducks, he had an idea!

When Little Matt arrived from school, Grandpa shared his idea with him.

"Little Matt, I found our peahen's nest in the brush today. I think we should take one of these duck eggs and place it in her nest. Perhaps she might take to sitting on the duck egg as her own."

"You mean the egg might hatch and our peahen will have a chick again?"

"Yes, it could be. It's certainly worth a try."

So early that evening, when the peahen was away from her nest, Little Matt gently placed a duck egg inside it.

Grandpa whispered, "Now we'll just have to wait to see what happens."

In the days that followed, they no longer saw or heard the peahen.

Little Matt asked, "Grandpa, where has our peahen gone?"

"Hmm," Grandpa replied. "Maybe she's flown away, or maybe ... just maybe ... "

"She's sitting on the duck egg!" cried Little Matt.

Several weeks passed. One afternoon, they heard a surprising sound.

Little Matt shouted, "Grandpa, look! It's our peahen! And she has a duckling following her!"

When mama peahen squawked, her little duckling answered, "Quack, quack, quack!"

Grandpa smiled in amazement.

Right away, the duckling found a puddle.

Grandpa said, "Soon the duckling will have oil on his feathers, and he'll be ready for his first swim."

"Oh, Grandpa, can we take them to the pond?" said Little Matt.

"That's a fine idea!" replied Grandpa.

And so at the right time, they led mama peahen and her duckling to the pond.

The duckling went straight into the water and began to paddle and float. He splashed and fluttered.

Little Matt shouted, "Grandpa, he's swimming!"

After a while, mama peahen squawked for her duckling to come back to her.

The duckling quickly paddled back to the shore.

Then Grandpa and Little Matt watched as mama peahen led her duckling all around the pond.

The End

Author's Note

Dear Readers,

Thank you for reading *Grandpa and the Peahen*, my first picture book. I got the idea for this story from an old friend, Ken, who had a peahen on his property. Creating this book took a lot of work, but it was definitely one of the most rewarding things I have done. I would greatly appreciate it if you would leave a review on my Amazon book page.

Sincerely,

Terry Ann Buchanan

Made in the USA
Coppell, TX
09 October 2020